INTERRUPTED BY GRACE

CHARLEY H WHITE

INTERRUPTED BY GRACE

For those I get the honor to love on earth:
Eric, Bentley & Hartley Ann
I love you more than buttered toast!!

For those I love on the other side of Heaven:
Eliza Jane, Walker Thomas & Clara Dean

Contents

Dear Reader

As I ponder the ways in which Jesus responded to the countless interruptions, whether it was healing the sick, raising the dead, or feeding the multitudes, I am struck by His willingness to stop, to meet people in their deepest need, and to offer them something far greater than they could have ever expected. Each of these moments serves as a powerful reminder that God is present in the interruptions of our lives.

As a mother, I understand the feeling of being interrupted, especially when it comes to raising my daughters. There are times when the demands of life seem overwhelming, when every moment is filled with tasks and responsibilities. But in those very moments, I believe God is inviting us to see interruptions not as inconveniences, but as opportunities for grace and transformation. Jesus didn't shy away from the interruptions He faced; He embraced them with compassion, and in doing so, He revealed the heart of God, the God who stops to care for the one, even in the midst of the many.

I pray that as you read this book, you will find encouragement in the interruptions of your own life. Just as Jesus met people in their moments of desperate need, He is ready and willing to meet you in yours. Whether it's in the quiet moments of motherhood or in the chaos of your day-to-day life, God is present, ready to show you His grace, His power, and His love.

With faith, hope, and love,
Charley H. White

Introduction

As mothers, there are days when life feels like a never-ending series of interruptions. We make plans, check off lists, and yearn for a moment of peace, only to be pulled in another direction—whether it's a child's cry, a phone call, or an unexpected task. And as a working mom, those interruptions only magnify at work, and make the ones we have to deal with at home seem much more intrusive, as the short hours I get to spend with my girls seem to be scattered tasks, sleepily done homework, and oftentimes screams of children who love each other very much who are very much yearning for their own space, their own time with their parents, and the solver of all those demands is usually: ME! How many times have we asked ourselves, *Will I ever finish a task without being interrupted?* Amidst the constant redirection, I rarely reflect on Jesus and the interruptions He experienced in His ministry, but in an effort to redirect my life toward my home being my largest ministry, I began delving into the ministry of Jesus, only to realize - during his short three year public ministry, the time he was trying to prepare his disciples hearts and minds for his crucifixion, resurrection and the start of the new church; he was interrupted CONSTANTLY!

The Gospels remind us that many of Jesus' miracles happened unexpectedly. His path was often interrupted by people in need, yet He never viewed these moments as hindrances to His mission. Instead, He saw each interruption as an opportunity to show grace. These moments are not unlike the interruptions we face as mothers. Each disruption we encounter offers a chance to extend grace, even in what may seem mundane or disruptive. In the same way, Jesus' interruptions were divine opportunities to reveal God's heart.

Imagine Jesus, knowing His time with His disciples was short. Each moment was precious, yet He allowed His teaching to be interrupted by people crossing His path at just the right time. The disciples must have struggled at times, feeling as though their time with Jesus was being interrupted. Perhaps they felt His attention should have been solely for them. But as they witnessed Jesus meeting the needs of those who sought Him, they began to understand that these interruptions were lessons on grace, faith, and inclusivity—preparing them for the ministry they would inherit.

The miracles of Jesus are more than displays of power; they are examples of His deep compassion. He never saw a need as a distraction. Instead, He paused, responded, and showed that each person mattered. As we read through these miracles, let's reflect on our own role as mothers and wives. How do we meet the needs of those around us, even when it means shifting our focus and surrendering our plans?

What if, instead of resisting interruptions, we welcomed them as divine appointments? What if we saw each disruption as a moment for grace, growth, and learning? In the smallest, most unexpected moments, we encounter God's love.

Jesus' life and ministry reveal a powerful truth: every interruption was an opportunity to extend grace and love. In the chapters ahead, we'll explore the miracles of Jesus, not only for their historical and cultural significance but for the lessons they teach us about grace, compassion, and the Kingdom of God.

I pray that as we reflect on these stories, we begin to see interruptions as holy moments, opportunities to extend grace and receive it. Just as Jesus turned every interruption into a chance to show grace, may we also see our interruptions as chances to experience God's grace and to extend it to others.

Through these interrupted lives, we honor God and find purpose in the unexpected. Jesus showed us how to live open to the work God is doing in us, especially when we least expect it. May we embrace our interrupted lives with grace, knowing that God is using these moments to shape us for His Kingdom.

At the end of each chapter, you will be called to
"Read, Ruminate & React"

Read

Take the time to carefully read the passage of Scripture highlighted in this chapter. As you read, try to imagine yourself in the story. Feel the emotions, experience the tension, and listen for God's voice in the words.

Ruminate

Ruminate means to chew on something, just like a cow chews its cud. Don't let the words pass by too quickly let them settle in your mind and spirit. Ask yourself questions like:

- What stands out to me in this passage?
- What emotions or thoughts stir in me?
- How does this story connect with my own experiences or struggles?

Take a moment to reflect on these things quietly, allowing God to reveal deeper truths.

React

How is God calling you to react? What next steps might He be inviting you into? You can react with prayer, an action, or a change of perspective. But whatever you do, let it be something that moves you closer to living out the bold, courageous faith that this woman with the issue of blood exemplified.

1

A Mother's Request

A Mother's Request

The wedding at Cana was meant to be a celebration, a joyous occasion filled with laughter, community, and the promise of new beginnings. Guests arrived in their finest attire, eager to witness the union of two families and share in the joy of the bride and groom. Yet, as with many moments in the life of Jesus, this gathering was about to be interrupted in a profound, grace-filled way, transforming the ordinary into the miraculous.

At the center of this interruption was a simple, yet urgent request from His mother, Mary. Although the conversation between Jesus and Mary is brief, the implications are deep. During the festivities, the wine ran out—a serious problem in a culture where hospitality was sacred, and feasts were cherished. To run out of wine was not only a mark of poor planning but a failure that could bring embarrassment to the families involved. In a society that valued honor and reputation, running out of wine could lead to social disgrace. This moment of need extended beyond a mere shortage; it was a crisis of communal honor.

This quiet, almost invisible miracle contrasts with the grander displays of Jesus' power, such as healing the sick or casting out demons. Here, there was no crowd clamoring for His attention, no shouts of desperation. Instead, Mary's faith moved her to turn to her Son, certain that He could meet the need. "Do whatever He tells you," she instructed the servants, her faith evident. For her, this moment was an interruption of grace—a quiet yet profound belief that her Son could perform what seemed impossible.

This passage speaks to the quiet strength of motherhood. In many ways, the daily work of a mother mirrors Mary's request. The small, unnoticed interruptions—the late-night glass of water, a comforting word, a moment to listen—are often unseen by the outside world. But they carry immense weight, symbolizing love, sacrifice, and trust. Mary's faith in Jesus wasn't simply about fixing a problem; it reflected a mother's deep trust in her child's ability to bring something miraculous to the mundane.

When Jesus responded to Mary, He did so with words that suggest a bigger purpose: "Woman, what does this have to do with me? My hour has not yet come." This response reflects a tension throughout His ministry. Jesus knew that the time for Him to reveal Himself as the Messiah would come, but it wasn't quite yet. And yet, moved by compassion and respect for His mother, He responded, honoring the need at hand.

This act defied expectations of what a miracle should look like, showing that grace can emerge in the quietest, most unexpected ways. Jesus instructed the servants to fill large stone jars with water—jars meant for ceremonial washing, according to Jewish law. These weren't mere containers; they were sacred vessels symbolizing purification. By transforming these jars from instruments of ritual cleansing into vessels of celebration, Jesus was hinting at a deeper mission. This was not just about fixing a social blunder; it was a revelation of grace. Through

His act, Jesus transformed the symbolic rituals of His people into a sign of divine abundance and joy.

When the water became wine, the celebration was renewed, and the feast continued. The steward, amazed by the quality of the wine, remarked, "You have kept the good wine until now." In a culture often marked by scarcity and limits, Jesus' miracle revealed that in His kingdom, there is always enough—more than enough. This abundance was a tangible reminder that grace is overflowing in God's kingdom, surpassing the expectations of the guests and reminding us that even our smallest needs can be met with divine generosity.

For those of us who are mothers, this moment resonates. We may not perform miracles, but we recognize the interruptions that come with caring for others. These moments—like the miracle at Cana—may not be marked by grandeur, yet they hold the potential for transformation. Jesus' act of quiet compassion in response to His mother's request invites us to see the interruptions of our lives as opportunities to meet others' needs with grace.

The cultural and social implications of this miracle extend even further. In Jesus' time, a wedding wasn't just a family affair; it was a communal event. The celebration crossed social boundaries, uniting the rich and the poor, the powerful and the marginalized. Wine was more than a drink; it symbolized joy, honor, and abundance. Running out of wine would have been more than an inconvenience; it would have dishonored the family and broken the social contract of hospitality. Jesus stepped in, not only preserving the family's dignity but redefining what abundance meant in His kingdom.

This miracle was a sign, a glimpse into the nature of the kingdom of God—a place where scarcity gives way to abundance, where every need is met, and where God's love overflows. By turning water into wine, Jesus foreshadowed the ultimate transformation His ministry would bring, shifting from the ritual cleansing of the old covenant to the joy and fullness of the new.

Reflecting on this, I think of how often grace comes to us quietly, in the interruptions we don't expect. Like the wedding at Cana, our lives are filled with moments when we are running low—on patience, strength, or hope. But in those moments, Jesus is present, ready to transform the ordinary into something beautiful. Just as He turns water into wine, He meets us in our need, offering a love that is abundant and life-giving.

As mothers, this story reminds us that our quiet acts of faith, compassion, and trust are powerful. They are moments where divine grace interrupts, renewing us and transforming our hearts. The wedding at Cana is more than a story of a miraculous sign; it's a reminder that God's grace is abundant, even in the places we least expect. In the kingdom of God, nothing is wasted, and every moment—every interruption—can become a testament to His endless love.

May we learn to welcome these interruptions with faith, as Mary did, trusting that Jesus can bring grace into even the simplest of needs. And as we do, may we see the abundance of His love overflow in our lives, transforming our ordinary moments into sacred experiences filled with the richness of His kingdom.

Read: John 2:1-11

Ruminate: Have you ever found yourself in a moment where you had no idea how things would work out, yet somehow, the solution came in an unexpected way? What did that teach you about trust?

How often do you, like the servants at the wedding, do what is asked of you without knowing the full plan? Can you think of a time when your obedience to a simple instruction led to an extraordinary result?

What does it mean to you that Jesus chose to perform His first miracle at a social event, one that involved people, celebration, and a common need? How might this shape your view of His involvement in your everyday life?

Do you find it difficult to see Jesus working in moments of perceived insignificance, like a wedding reception? What would it look like if you truly believed He is active in every part of your life, not just the "big" moments?

React:

Take a moment to reflect on the areas of your life where you feel the pressure of needing a solution, whether it's a personal challenge or something you're walking through with someone else. Jesus met the needs at the wedding without fanfare, but the outcome was a demonstration of His power. What do you need to place before Him today, trusting that even the seemingly small requests or moments can be opportunities for His miraculous grace to shine? Take time to listen for what He's asking you to do, and then respond in faith, no matter how unlikely the outcome may seem.

2

Faith from the Unlikely

Faith from the Unlikely

Reflecting on the strength it takes each day to walk in faith as a mother, wife, and believer, I am reminded that faith can emerge from the most unexpected places, and sometimes through the most unlikely of people. The story of the centurion and his servant is a profound example of this truth—a story where humility and unexpected faith converged to reveal God's grace.

This centurion was a Roman officer, a figure of authority and command, yet he was also a man marked by remarkable compassion and humility. Serving in Capernaum, a Jewish city on the shores of the Sea of Galilee, he was a daily reminder of Roman occupation for the Jewish people. His position set him apart socially, culturally, and religiously; he was a Gentile and a foreigner, embedded in a community that viewed him as an outsider. And yet, his faith would come to interrupt Jesus' ministry and open the eyes of those who witnessed it to something extraordinary.

The centurion's request was simple but profound: he sought healing for his servant. In Roman society, servants were typically viewed as property, replaceable at best. But this centurion's plea reflected genuine care and respect for his servant, a compassion that would have surprised the people of his rank and certainly the Jewish observers of the time. His compassion set him apart, but it was his understanding of Jesus' authority that brought him even closer to the heart of God's kingdom.

As Jesus moved through the bustling streets of Capernaum, surrounded by those eager to hear Him teach, this Gentile approached—a Roman officer, yet remarkably aware of who Jesus truly was. The centurion's response to Jesus was grounded not in pride or obligation but in a humility that surpassed even the faith of those closest to Jesus. When he finally spoke, he did so with a profound sense of reverence:

"Lord, I am not worthy that you should come under my roof; but only speak a word, and my servant will be healed" (Matthew 8:8, NKJV).

His words were powerful. The centurion did not ask Jesus to come to his home, nor did he ask for a physical sign. Instead, he understood and trusted the authority of Jesus' words alone. This Gentile understood what even those who walked with Jesus struggled to grasp: that Jesus' power was not bound by rituals or symbols, nor by physical proximity. His word alone was enough.

For the disciples and the crowd, this moment must have been stunning. The Jewish people had long anticipated a Messiah to deliver them, yet here was a Gentile soldier, part of the empire that oppressed them, showing a faith that Jesus declared to be greater than any He had found in Israel. Turning to the crowd, Jesus proclaimed,

"I have not found such great faith, not even in Israel" (Matthew 8:10, NKJV).

This statement must have resounded in the hearts of all who heard it. By praising the centurion's faith, Jesus showed that the boundaries of God's kingdom would extend beyond cultural or ethnic limits. This Gentile, whom many saw as an outsider, embodied a faith that would inspire and challenge all who witnessed it. For the early church, this moment served as a potent reminder: the kingdom of God would be open to all who believed, regardless of background or social standing.

The centurion's story teaches us that faith is not about religious heritage, social status, or proximity to tradition. It is about belief in the power and authority of Jesus. The centurion's trust was rooted in a simple understanding of Jesus' divine authority, a faith that allowed him to transcend cultural barriers and see clearly who Jesus was. He approached Jesus with a profound humility, recognizing that His word alone held power to heal and restore.

This story calls us to examine our own approach to God. We may feel, at times, that our own backgrounds or circumstances make us less worthy of drawing near to Him. But this story reminds us that Jesus welcomes all who approach Him with genuine faith, no matter how unlikely they may seem. The centurion's faith was not based on religious knowledge or status, but on a deep, simple trust in Jesus. It is a testament to the boundless reach of God's compassion and power, extending to all who dare to believe.

Through this interruption, Jesus revealed a new perspective on belonging in God's kingdom—a kingdom defined not by earthly borders but by faith. The centurion's faith, unexpected and bold, became a witness to the boundless nature of God's grace. His story reminds us that Jesus listens to all who come to Him with humble hearts, regardless of where they come from or how far they feel from belonging.

In this event, we witness an interruption that transcends cultural, social, and religious boundaries, revealing the heart of God's kingdom. Just as Jesus stopped to hear the plea of a Roman officer, He pauses to hear our prayers, welcoming our faith even when it comes from unlikely places. This story stands as a reminder that each time we approach Him with genuine belief, we join in a legacy of grace—a legacy that began in unexpected places and continues in the lives of all who seek Him. May we, like the centurion, approach Jesus with humility and confidence, trusting in His authority and His endless capacity to extend grace to us all.

Read: Matthew 8:5-13, Luke 7:1-10, Acts 10:34-35, Romans 10:12-13, Acts 15:6-29

Ruminate: How does the centurion's faith challenge traditional ideas about who is "worthy" in God's eyes?

What social or cultural boundaries in your own life might need to be reexamined considering this story?

In what ways does this narrative call us to extend compassion and faith beyond our own community or background?

React: This week, consider ways to reach across cultural or social divides in faith and compassion. Emulate the centurion's humility by seeking ways to honor the faith of others, even if they come from backgrounds different from your own. Share an act of kindness with someone outside your usual circle, showing the love of Christ in a tangible way. Let the centurion's story inspire a deeper faith and a commitment to embracing all whom God may place in your path, seeing them as God does—worthy of love and grace.

3

The Faith of Friends

The Faith of Friends

In the rhythms of life, interruptions often feel like inconveniences, breaking into our neatly laid plans. I know how hard it can be to pause when we're focused on what needs doing, the tasks and to-do lists of each day. But sometimes, these interruptions are like a gust of unexpected grace, changing us in ways we didn't even realize we needed. This story of the paralyzed man and his friends who carried him is one such story—a moment when faith-filled friends stopped everything, in pursuit of grace they knew would bring healing.

The scene was alive with expectation. Jesus had returned to Capernaum, and word had spread like a fire on a dry field. Crowds poured in, all seeking a glimpse, a word, a miracle from the Teacher who spoke of heaven with a voice like thunder and whose touch had the power to heal. In a house packed wall-to-wall with eager faces, many likely stood shoulder-to-shoulder, unable to see Him clearly, yet holding onto the hope that just being near Him was enough.

Outside, a group of friends gathered around a mat where one of their own lay still, unable to walk. They must have shared years of laughter and hardship, bonds formed through countless moments of loyalty and love. But recently, their friend's life had been marked by stillness, his body unresponsive to his own will. They had likely watched him try, again and again, to move and to walk, yet each attempt was met with frustration and loss. But today, news reached them: Jesus was back, and with Him, the chance for healing.

Imagine the weight they lifted, not just their friend's body but the emotional weight of hope and disappointment that had been their shared burden. This was more than a practical task; it was a journey of love and of friendship. With steady arms and unrelenting faith, they set out for Jesus, carrying with them every ounce of hope they had stored up through months, maybe years, of waiting and wondering if their friend would ever walk again.

As they arrived at the house, their hearts must have sunk at the sight of the overflowing crowd. A wall of people, all equally desperate, blocked the door and filled the yard. There was no clear way to enter, no path to the Teacher they so urgently sought. In that moment, many might have turned back, discouraged. They had done all they could, had tried to bring their friend where the healing was, and the door was closed. But not these friends. With eyes that looked not to the crowd but to the rooftops, they felt a daring resolve. Perhaps they remembered the ways God had provided in the past, or perhaps they felt a boldness born of pure love. Either way, they made the bold choice to climb up, their hearts pounding as they hauled their friend to the roof and began to pull away tiles.

In the middle of that packed house, as Jesus spoke words of life to those gathered around, a strange noise from above must have paused the room's hushed awe. A scraping, lifting, falling of dust and bits of roof rained down, and the crowd looked up, startled, to see a crack in the ceiling widening into a hole. Then, to everyone's amazement, they watched as a mat was slowly lowered down, right into the middle of them all.

Imagine Jesus, seeing this group of friends through the breaking light above, their faces beaming with hope, eyes fixed on Him with a bold, childlike trust. They had interrupted everything. This was no small disruption, but the heart of Jesus was moved by the sight. Here was an interruption of grace. He looked upon the paralyzed man with love, His gaze taking in not only the man's suffering but the extraordinary devotion and courage of his friends. Jesus saw their faith—the faith that had persisted, climbed, pulled back roof tiles, and lowered their friend into His presence.

But the miracle He offered was not the one they had expected. Looking at the man, He did not start with physical healing. Instead, Jesus said, "Son, thy sins be forgiven thee." In those words, Jesus reached deeper than the man's physical need; He saw his heart, his soul's longing for freedom from guilt and burden, and met him there first. It's a maternal moment, a moment that reminds me of when we tend to wounds unseen, seeing not only what is needed but the deeper ache underneath. Jesus knew this man's pain was not only in his legs but in his spirit, and He gave healing where it mattered most.

The religious leaders standing nearby were taken aback. This pronouncement of forgiveness was radical, offensive even. In their minds, forgiveness was something bound to the temple, dependent on rituals and sacrifices. Who was this man who dared to forgive sins as though He had divine authority? But Jesus perceived their thoughts, challenging their skepticism. "Which is easier?" He asked, "to say, 'Your sins are forgiven,' or to say, 'Rise, take up your mat and walk'?"

With that, He turned to the man and declared, "Arise, take up thy bed, and go thy way." And in that moment, strength filled the man's body as he rose, picked up his mat, and walked out of that crowded home. The friends who had carried him there witnessed his first steps in what must have felt like years—a sight that must have brought tears to their eyes, a release of joy and relief they had longed to experience.

In their determination, in their relentless pursuit of Jesus, these friends gave their paralyzed companion not just a chance at healing, but a moment when grace interrupted his life, changed it, and redefined it forever. Their faith was unshakeable, a testament to the kind of love that is patient and long-suffering, that bears all things, believes all things, and hopes all things. In their actions, they modeled the very heart of God—an unrelenting love that moves mountains, or in this case, roofs, to make a way for healing.

This story doesn't just tell us about healing, but about the faith that sees past obstacles and persists in bringing us to God. These friends remind us of the way a mother's love persists, the way a friend's loyalty holds steady, the way faith can transform our burdens when we bring them into Jesus' presence. And Jesus, in turn, shows us that He is not just a teacher or a healer, but the very embodiment of God's grace, willing to be interrupted for the sake of one soul in need.

We, too, are invited to press through the crowds of doubt and discouragement, to push through our obstacles, and to bring our burdens to Jesus, trusting that He sees beyond our immediate needs to the deeper places of our hearts. Just as those friends wouldn't leave until they had placed their friend at Jesus' feet, we're reminded that God's grace is not held back by obstacles. In fact, He welcomes the faithful interruptions of those who come to Him in love and desperation.

This moment, like so many interruptions in Jesus' ministry, shattered expectations. It showed that grace is accessible not only to the outwardly religious or the ritually pure but to anyone who seeks Jesus with a sincere heart. And as He looked upon the man, He didn't see a mere interruption in His schedule but a soul in need, a life ready for transformation.

As we take this story to heart, may we find courage in these friends who didn't hesitate to break through a roof to reach Jesus. May we be reminded that our faith, our love, and our determination can move obstacles, bringing ourselves and those we love closer to the grace that Jesus is so ready to give. And may we see that in every interruption, every moment when life does not go as planned, there is often a grace waiting to meet us, a reminder that in Him, every interruption can become an invitation for grace to break through.

Read: Mark 2:1-12, Psalm 103:2-3, Isaiah 53:5

Ruminate:

What areas in my life feel paralyzed or in need of healing? How might my faith—active and unwavering—help bring these needs to Jesus?

Are there social or personal "barriers" I need to overcome in my faith journey? How can I take active steps to seek Jesus?

In what ways can I help carry others to Jesus, as the friends did for the paralyzed man?

React:

Consider how you can make space for Jesus in your daily life, even in interruptions. Actively bring your own needs and those of others before Him in prayer, trusting that His response will go beyond the physical to meet the deepest needs of the heart. Let this story inspire you to be relentless in your faith, to seek God's grace for both yourself and those around you, regardless of obstacles.

4

A Miracle in the House

A Miracle in the House

As the sun began to dip below the horizon in Capernaum, the streets began to quiet, and the day's dust settled in the air. The evening breeze brought a coolness, a welcome respite after a long, bustling day. But for one household in the city—the home of Simon Peter—peace was a distant hope. Inside, Peter's mother-in-law lay feverish, gripped by an illness that had refused to relent, leaving the household concerned, waiting, and praying.

In the first-century world, a fever was far more than just a temporary ailment. Without modern medicine or antibiotics, it was a harbinger of uncertainty. A fever could signal anything from a mild discomfort to the beginning of something far more serious. Families lived in constant anxiety when illness struck, especially when it affected a woman, whose role was so deeply intertwined with the rhythm of daily life. Her sickness wasn't just a physical burden—it had ripple effects throughout the entire household. The heart of the home, the one who kept things in order, was now rendered powerless to fulfill the responsibilities that gave her purpose.

Peter's mother-in-law, like many women of her time, would have found deep significance in her work within the home. Preparing meals, welcoming guests, and ensuring that the household was cared for—these weren't just duties; they were part of her identity. In a time and culture where women often had little control over their public lives, their role within the home was where their influence lay. To be stricken by illness was to lose not just one's health, but one's ability to serve, to care, to be the backbone of the family.

And so, when Jesus entered Peter's home that evening, it wasn't just another visitor walking through the door. It was a moment of quiet desperation, a final hope that perhaps, in His mercy, He could change what seemed inevitable. Peter, having already witnessed the power of Jesus to heal and to cast out demons, could only hope that Jesus would bring the same mercy and authority into this intimate, humble setting. This wasn't a public spectacle—it wasn't a grand healing in the streets or in a crowded synagogue—but a quiet intervention in a private home.

There was a subtle tension in the air when Jesus walked into the room. Peter's wife, perhaps, hovered in the background, watching with concern as Jesus approached her mother. The disciples were present too, still in awe of everything Jesus had done, but this moment was different. This wasn't just another public display of power—it was personal. It involved someone they knew, someone whose care had meant so much to their lives.

Without hesitation, Jesus approached the woman lying in bed. She was weak, her body trembling, her strength drained. She may not have even fully recognized who had entered her home, but Jesus stood beside her nonetheless. In an act of both profound tenderness and divine authority, He reached out and took her by the hand.

Luke's Gospel notes that Jesus "rebuked the fever" (Luke 4:39, KJV), speaking to it with the same authority He used to silence unclean spirits. The very word "rebuke" is significant—it suggests an authority so strong that even sickness must obey. This wasn't just a simple healing;

it was a confrontation with the forces that had stripped this woman of her strength and vitality. And in an instant, the fever left her.

There is so much to take in from this seemingly simple moment. For Peter's mother-in-law, this wasn't just the restoration of her body, it was the reclamation of her identity, her place, her purpose. As soon as the fever left, she immediately rose and began to serve them (Mark 1:31, KJV). This was not an ordinary act of hospitality; this was a woman stepping back into her calling, a woman reclaiming her dignity. In a society where a woman's worth was often tied to her ability to serve and provide for others, Jesus gave her the gift of being able to fulfill that role once again. The fever that had sidelined her, that had robbed her of her ability to care, was gone, and she was restored to herself.

This act of healing was more than just physical. Jesus, with His touch, didn't just heal her body—He healed her standing in the family, in the community, and before God. In an era where women's roles were often confined to the private realm, Jesus showed that no act of service was beneath His notice. His ministry wasn't concerned with status or outward appearances. It was about seeing people for who they were, for what they needed, and for what they could offer to the world.

In Jewish culture, hospitality wasn't just a courtesy; it was a deeply ingrained tradition, a moral and spiritual obligation. The Torah recounts Abraham's hospitality to the three visitors under the oaks of Mamre (Genesis 18:1-8, KJV), and this act of hospitality became one of the cornerstones of Jewish values. So, when Peter's mother-in-law rose from her sickbed and immediately began to serve, she wasn't just attending to the needs of Jesus and His disciples. She was stepping into a long lineage of women who had honored God through their service, who had opened their homes and hearts to others. She was participating in a sacred act, a tradition that spanned generations.

For the early church, this story would carry profound significance. The idea that Jesus would pause His public ministry to heal someone in such a private, personal setting would come to define the early church's understanding of ministry. This wasn't about grandeur or recognition; it was about meeting people where they were, in their homes, in their ordinary lives. The early Christians would come to see that the presence of Christ could fill any space—not just temples or synagogues, but homes and humble places, too.

And for women, especially those who found their roles limited to the private sphere, this miracle was revolutionary. Jesus didn't just acknowledge Peter's mother-in-law as a sick woman in need of physical healing. He saw her as a person with a purpose, a woman with a calling that extended far beyond her illness. In an age where women's contributions were often ignored or minimized, Jesus elevated her. He met her in her moment of suffering, restored her, and gave her the ability to serve once again. This act of healing was an affirmation of her worth, a reminder that her role was significant, even in a society that often overlooked her.

For the rest of the disciples, this act of quiet healing would have been deeply revealing. They had seen Jesus heal the crowds, cast out demons, and perform mighty acts of power in front of throngs of people. But here, in the privacy of a home, Jesus demonstrated that the most sacred encounters didn't always need a crowd. His presence wasn't confined to temples or public settings. It was just as powerful in the quiet moments, in the unseen acts of love and restoration.

For us, the story of Peter's mother-in-law offers deep encouragement. It reminds us that Jesus doesn't overlook the small acts of service, the quiet moments of grace. Even when we are at our lowest, even when life feels interrupted by illness, exhaustion, or hardship, Jesus sees us. He meets us where we are—right in the middle of our own struggles—and in His mercy, He restores not only our physical health but also our sense of purpose and worth.

As women, as mothers, we often find ourselves in roles that demand constant care and service, much of which goes unnoticed by the world. Yet, in this simple miracle, Jesus affirms that no act of service is too small, no role too insignificant. Whether we are serving our families, our communities, or simply showing up each day with love and grace, Jesus sees. And just as He honored the service of Peter's mother-in-law, He honors our service, too.

In our busy lives, filled with constant demands and interruptions, we may sometimes feel that our work goes unnoticed. We may become discouraged, wondering if the small, everyday acts of care are truly meaningful. But this story reminds us that Jesus sees it all. Every meal prepared, every word of encouragement spoken, every moment of love shared—these acts are seen by Him, and He values them deeply.

This miracle, small in scale but monumental in its implications, calls us to see our interruptions as opportunities for grace. Whether it's a moment of quiet compassion in our own home, a word of encouragement to a friend, or an act of service to a stranger, we can be assured that Jesus is present. He doesn't wait for grand, public moments to show His grace. He enters our homes, our lives, our moments of struggle, and He transforms them with His healing touch.

As we reflect on this story, may we be reminded that no matter where we are—whether in the middle of a bustling crowd or in the quiet of our own home—Jesus is present. He sees us, He meets us in our need, and He brings grace to the ordinary, transforming even the smallest acts into moments of divine encounter. And in those interruptions, we can find the opportunity to serve Him, just as Peter's mother-in-law did, with gratitude and love.

Read: Luke 4:38-39, Mark 1:29-31, Acts 2:46, Genesis 18:1-8, KJV

Ruminate: In what ways have you experienced interruptions that turned into opportunities for growth or grace?

How can you see Jesus' compassion for Peter's mother-in-law mirrored in His regard for our roles today, whether public or private?

How might this story inspire you to serve others in your own home, seeing each act of kindness as an opportunity to honor God?

React: Consider how you might extend grace to someone in need this week, recognizing that every encounter—even the quiet ones—can become a moment to share God's love. Seek opportunities to serve others, whether within your family, among friends, or even in unexpected interruptions, trusting that each act of kindness reflects God's Kingdom..

5

Interruption of Worship

Interruption of Worship

The narrow, bustling streets of Capernaum were alive with conversation, expectation, and a hint of mystery as word spread that Jesus was nearby. The city, brimming with anticipation, had seen its fair share of miracles, yet each time He returned, the excitement was no less than before. Every time He walked through the streets, the hope that swelled in the hearts of the people made the air feel heavier, as though it could carry the weight of their collective prayers.

In this small town, where life moved at a slow and steady pace, the arrival of Jesus was like a breath of fresh air. Wherever He went, crowds followed—men, women, and children alike, each eager to see the One who spoke with such wisdom and authority. They came to hear His teachings, to witness His miracles, and to be near the One whom they believed might hold the power to change everything. But today, on this particular evening, the scene would unfold in a way that was wholly unexpected.

The setting was the house of Simon, a Pharisee, whose home was likely a spacious, well-kept courtyard structure, built with all the careful attention to detail that would have been customary for a man of his stature. Simon's house was more than just a place of residence; it was a setting for rituals, social gatherings, and moments of theological discussion. It was a place where men of influence met to talk about the Scriptures, and where tradition and propriety were honored with every detail.

On this evening, Simon had invited Jesus to dine, perhaps out of curiosity, or perhaps to assess for himself whether the rumors surrounding this rabbi were true. His gathering was one of men of influence—Pharisees who were accustomed to the subtleties of conversation and the weight of judgment. They watched each word Jesus spoke, ready to dissect His every action, seeking to uncover any flaw, any inconsistency, or any reason to discredit Him.

But the evening took an unexpected turn when she entered the room—uninvited, unnoticed at first by the others, but utterly impossible to ignore once she was there. She was a woman known to many in the town—labeled as a sinner, marked by her past. She carried a reputation that had made her an outsider, cast aside by the community that once knew her. The title "sinner" had followed her like a shadow, one that no amount of time or repentance could erase. Perhaps she had been a prostitute; perhaps her life had been filled with choices she had not made freely, but rather out of desperation, her sins now casting a long shadow over her every action.

In her time of need, she had sought refuge with Jesus, whose reputation preceded Him. She had heard about the miracles, the healings, the love and compassion He offered to those society considered undeserving. She may have been cautious, unsure of what to expect, but one thing was clear: she had come to Him because she knew He was the only one who could offer her the healing she longed for—not just of her body, but of her heart.

As she moved quietly through the door, she entered a room full of men who, for all their knowledge and devotion to the law, lacked the warmth and grace that Jesus so freely offered. Her presence would have been unsettling for them, for she was a woman of scandal, her actions breaking every rule of propriety. But she did not hesitate. She moved with a purpose that only the truly broken can understand, and her eyes were fixed on Jesus. She had come to find the grace she had been searching for, the kind of grace that interrupts everything, that stops the world in its tracks.

Without a word, she approached Him from behind and knelt at His feet, overwhelmed by the weight of her past and the grace that called her forward. Her tears fell—silent but heavy with emotion—as she let them spill over His dusty feet, each tear carrying years of sorrow, regret, and longing. Her hands, trembling with humility, reached down to wipe the tears away, using her hair—an act that no woman in her right mind would do in public. It was scandalous, intimate even, yet it was the only way she knew to express the depth of her gratitude and devotion. In that act, she poured out everything she had—her sorrow, her love, her worship.

The room grew still as she anointed His feet with perfume. The alabaster box she held contained precious ointment, a luxury she likely had acquired through her past life—a past that she now sought to leave behind. This perfume was not just a symbol of her old life; it was her offering, her act of worship. She cracked open the box, releasing the fragrance into the room, and in that moment, every eye was on her. It was an interruption—an interruption to the carefully arranged dinner, to the expected flow of conversation, to the dignity of the men gathered there. But it was also an interruption of grace.

For the Pharisees in the room, her actions were beyond offensive. She was a sinner, a woman of shame. Simon's judgment was immediate, and he thought to himself, "If this man were truly a prophet, He would know who this woman is." To Simon, her past was all that mattered. Her sins, her mistakes, her shame—they were what defined her, and he could not understand how Jesus could allow such a woman to touch Him. Yet Jesus, seeing the silent judgment in Simon's heart, did not respond in anger or condemnation. Instead, He responded with grace, with a story that would turn everything on its head.

Jesus spoke of two debtors—one who owed a great deal, the other a small amount. When neither could repay, both debts were forgiven. Jesus asked Simon, "Which one will love the creditor more?" Simon, though uncomfortable, answered honestly, "I suppose the one who was forgiven more." Jesus turned to the woman, still kneeling at His feet, and gently rebuked Simon, pointing out the woman's love as the truest form of worship.

"You see this woman?" He asked Simon. "I entered your house; you gave Me no water for My feet, but she has washed My feet with her tears and wiped them with her hair. You gave Me no kiss, but this woman has not ceased to kiss My feet since I came in. You did not anoint My head with oil, but this woman has anointed My feet with ointment." (Luke 7:44-46, KJV)

In that simple statement, Jesus laid bare the true meaning of devotion—humility, love, and gratitude. He acknowledged the woman's act as the truest expression of faith, for she understood what it meant to be forgiven, to be loved, and to be seen by the One who could heal her brokenness. Jesus did not reject her past; He welcomed her into His grace, interrupting her life with His love in the most tender way.

Finally, Jesus turned to the woman and offered her peace: "Thy sins are forgiven. Thy faith hath saved thee; go in peace." (Luke 7:48, KJV) In these words, Jesus released her from the weight of her past, offering her a new identity. She was no longer the sinner who had been cast aside by society. She was a woman forgiven, loved, and redeemed.

For the early church, this woman's story was one of radical love and grace. It was a story of worship that transcended societal norms and boundaries, a reminder that Jesus did not come for the righteous, but for the brokenhearted. Her story echoed in the hearts of the first believers, challenging them to see faith not as a matter of status or ritual, but as a relationship with a Savior who sees the heart.

Her bold act of love, her interruption of grace, became a model for early Christians who would gather in homes and share meals in secret. They, too, would find their faith in acts of love that disrupted the ordinary, breaking down barriers between God and His people.

In her act of worship, this woman's story teaches us that it is often in the most unexpected moments—those interruptions in our daily lives—that we encounter God's grace. She showed us that when we bring all that we have, even the broken pieces, before Jesus, He meets us with the love that transcends our past, our mistakes, and our shame. In offering all we have, we find peace that only He can give—a peace that surpasses all understanding, one that transforms even the most ordinary moments into sacred encounters with the Divine.

Read: Luke 7:36-50, Matthew 26:6-13, Isaiah 1:18, Romans 5:8

Ruminate: How does the woman's radical act of worship challenge your understanding of how we are to approach Jesus?

What does Jesus' response to Simon reveal about our tendency to judge others by outward appearances, while neglecting the deeper matters of the heart?

In what ways might we withhold our worship or devotion because of shame, past mistakes, or fear of societal judgment?

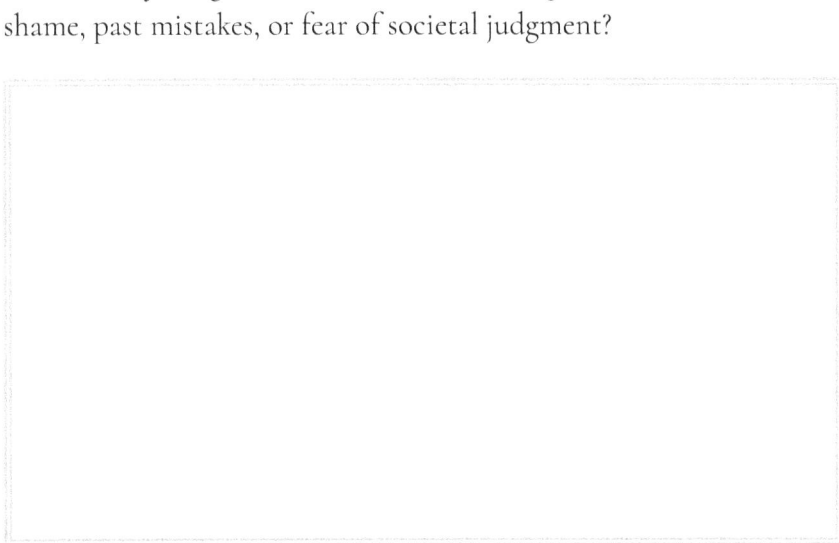

React: Take a moment to reflect on areas of your life where you may feel unworthy of God's grace or hesitant to approach Him with the fullness of your love. Consider how you might honor God with a bold act of worship—something that transcends comfort zones or societal expectations. This could be through prayer, service to others, or by dedicating your time and resources in a way that truly honors Him. Let your love for Jesus be genuine, unreserved, and unashamed, trusting that His grace is greater than any past mistake. Remember that He welcomes you, just as He welcomed the woman with the alabaster box, with love and compassion beyond measure.

6

⁓⁂⁓

Desperate Hope

Desperate Hope

Amid a bustling crowd, Jesus walked the narrow, crowded streets of Capernaum, His every step closely watched. The air was thick with anticipation, the city alive with the sounds of voices—some curious, some hopeful, and some skeptical. People pressed in from all sides, eager to witness His miracles, to hear His teachings, or perhaps to simply touch the robe of this remarkable teacher and healer. It appears every soul within a mile radius had come to see the man who was disrupting the very fabric of their understanding of God and life. The expectation was palpable.

But among the masses, one woman stood out—not because she was anyone special in the eyes of the world, but because of the quiet, desperate hope that burned in her chest. For twelve long years, she had suffered in silence, both physically and socially. The bleeding that marked her every moment of existence had not only stolen her health but had also stolen her place in the community. It had severed her relationships, her spiritual life, and her sense of identity. In a society governed by the strict laws of purity and cleanliness, her condition rendered her ritually unclean. She could not enter the synagogue. She could not be touched by another without defiling them. She was, in essence, invisible to the world around her—a woman marked by an affliction that made her untouchable.

Her life had become an unending cycle of pain and isolation. She had sought healing through every possible means, spending all her money on physicians who promised a cure, only to leave her more destitute and with no hope of a cure. Each failed attempt brought with it a deeper sense of failure and frustration. The dreams of a cure, of restored community, of simple human connection, had faded. What was once a life filled with possibility had turned into a life of solitude and despair. She had become a shadow of the woman she once was, her identity tethered to her sickness and her status as an outcast.

Yet on this particular day, something shifted in her spirit. The same crowd that pressed in on Jesus was not just a sea of strangers to her—it was a beacon of hope. Word had spread that Jesus was nearby. This man, who healed the sick, raised the dead, and welcomed sinners, had become a legend in their midst. Though she had heard the rumors, it was only now, in the swirling chaos of the crowd, that she dared to believe the impossible: perhaps He could heal her too. Perhaps He, the Rabbi of the people, could make her whole again.

She had heard about Him—how He had touched the leper without hesitation, how He had dined with sinners, how He had defied the cultural norms and expectations of the religious elite. In Him, there was mercy and compassion that made no sense according to the strict rules of the law. And in that moment, as Jesus walked through the streets of Capernaum, something in her heart told her: *This is my chance*.

But how could she approach Him? She was unclean. She had been taught all her life that her condition made her less than, unworthy of God's attention. She was not to be touched, nor was she to touch anyone else. And yet, there was a stirring in her that told her, if only she could touch the hem of His garment, she might be healed. She knew the rules, and she knew she was breaking them, but the desperation inside her outweighed the shame. She had already been rejected by society; what did she have left to lose?

As the crowd pressed in tighter, she moved carefully, silently, slipping through the throng with a boldness born of desperation and faith. No one noticed her at first—how could they? She was just another face in the crowd. And so, she pushed forward, hoping that if she could just reach Him, if she could just touch His robe, maybe—just maybe—her suffering would end.

Finally, she was there, close enough to stretch out her trembling hand. She hesitated for a split second, unsure if she dared to risk it. The moment she brushed her fingers against the fringe of His garment, everything changed. A warmth, a surge of power, radiated from His robe and into her very being. She felt the pain, the heaviness, the years of bleeding—all disappeared in an instant. Her body, once burdened with affliction, was now whole. Her strength returned, her heart lightened, and for the first time in years, she breathed freely.

She knew she had been healed. The crowd continued to move around her, oblivious to the miracle that had just taken place. But Jesus, ever aware of the needs of His people, stopped. He turned and asked, "Who touched Me?"

His disciples, who were caught up in the swirl of the crowd, were confused. "Master, the crowd presses on You from every side, and yet You ask, 'Who touched Me?'" they responded, bewildered by His question. The moment seemed like just another instance of Jesus' teaching, but to Him, it was something far more significant. He had felt power leave Him—a transfer of grace, a response to a touch that held the full weight of her faith.

The woman, her heart racing, could no longer remain hidden. She had touched Him in secret, but the healing was no secret to Jesus. With fear and trembling, she approached Him, knowing that her uncleanliness made her worthy of condemnation. She expected a rebuke, perhaps a public declaration of her violation of the law. But instead, she found something she had never anticipated: compassion.

As she knelt before Him, Jesus looked at her with eyes full of understanding, not judgment. "Daughter," He said, His voice tender and full of love, *"be of good comfort: thy faith hath made thee whole; go in peace"* (Luke 8:48, KJV).

The word "daughter" must have pierced her heart in a way nothing else could. In that moment, Jesus gave her not only physical healing but spiritual and social restoration as well. She had been cast out, deemed unworthy, but Jesus, with one word, gave her a place—a new identity. She was no longer the woman with the issue of blood; she was His daughter. No longer a social outcast, she was welcomed into the family of God.

This moment was no small thing. The woman's faith had interrupted Jesus' journey, yes, but in doing so, she revealed the very heart of His mission. The world may have seen her as a disruption, a distraction, but in Jesus' eyes, she was the reason He came—to heal the broken, to restore the lost, and to bring grace to those who thought they had none. Her act of faith was a testimony of the kingdom of God—a kingdom where no one is excluded, where grace flows freely, and where healing is not just physical but emotional, social, and spiritual.

Her story is not just the story of a woman who was healed of her affliction; it is the story of a woman whose life was completely transformed by an act of grace. She had been shunned by society, labeled by her condition, but in one encounter with Jesus, everything changed. Her healing was an interruption in His journey, but it was the interruption of grace that knows no boundaries, that heals not just the body but the soul.

As the early church would soon learn, this woman's story would be a model of bold faith and extravagant grace. Her willingness to defy the social norms, to approach Jesus in her brokenness, was a picture of the gospel. She did not wait to be made clean before coming to Jesus;

she came in her brokenness, and He healed her. In doing so, He proclaimed to all who would listen that the kingdom of God is open to all.

The healing of the woman with the issue of blood was not just a miracle of physical restoration; it was a powerful declaration of God's heart for the marginalized, the broken, and the outcasts. It was a reminder that grace is not earned but given freely to all who seek it with faith. In this one moment, Jesus broke down barriers, not just of illness, but of culture, tradition, and societal expectations. Her faith revealed the depth of God's love, a love that would not be contained by tradition or law but would overflow to all who would come to Him, no matter their past.

This story, and the miracle it represents, echoes throughout the life of the early church, reminding believers that Jesus' ministry was not about adhering to societal norms, but about bringing grace to those who needed it most. The woman, once invisible and rejected, became a model of faith and an example of the transformative power of God's love.

Read: Mark 5:28-29

Ruminate: When you face feelings of inadequacy or exhaustion as a mother, how do you find the strength to reach out to Jesus in faith?

The woman had to press through a crowd of obstacles to reach Jesus. What "crowds" or obstacles do you face in your life that make it hard to reach out to God for healing, peace, or strength?

How does Jesus' response to the woman encourage you in your own faith journey? How might this story help you reframe moments of personal struggle as opportunities to experience Jesus' grace?

React: When you find yourself in a season of desperation or struggle, remember that Jesus sees you. Like the woman, take a bold step in faith, even if it feels impossible. Reach out to Him in prayer, trusting that His grace is sufficient, and His healing power is available. Don't allow the obstacles in your life to stop you from seeking Him—press through the crowds of doubt and fear and experience the transformative grace He offers.

7

A Father's Faith, A Mother's Loss

A Father's Faith, A Mother's Loss

As a mother, there are few things more devastating than hearing that your child is sick, and even fewer things more heartbreaking than the thought of losing them. The intense, helpless feeling that fills your heart when you know there is nothing you can do is unlike any other. I've often wondered how much deeper the pain would be if the sickness were terminal. What would it be like to know that, despite all your love, all your care, and all your efforts, you might not be able to save the life of the one you love most? I can't imagine how Jairus, a father, must have felt that day as he watched his little girl slip away from him. Her life, once full of laughter and love, now hung by a fragile thread. The innocence of her childhood, so full of potential, had turned into a battlefield where life and death collided.

In those moments, a parent is thrust into a place of absolute helplessness. As a mother, I can feel the ache in Jairus' chest, the gut-wrenching longing to hold his child, to do whatever it took to bring her back to life. But the helplessness must have been even more suffocating for him, not only because of the illness but also because of his position in society. Jairus was a ruler of the synagogue—a man of influence, respect, and religious authority. In a community where reputation and social standing were of the utmost importance, he was a man of great stature. He was seen as a leader, a pillar of the faith. But in that moment, when his daughter lay dying, none of that mattered.

All the wealth, power, and influence in the world couldn't save her. His status could not bring her back to health. His religious knowledge, his understanding of the law, had not prepared him for this kind of heartbreak. There was no manual for how to handle the loss of a child, no sermon that could console him in this unimaginable moment. What could he do? Where could he turn? The world had offered him nothing, and no one could help him now.

In the face of all his status, the only thing Jairus had left was faith. Faith in something, someone, outside the realm of his understanding. The faith to believe that in the midst of his despair, a miracle might still be possible. He had heard the stories of Jesus—of the miracles, the healings, the impossible made possible. He had seen the crowds, witnessed the buzz of excitement that surrounded this rabbi, this teacher. And now, in his darkest hour, Jairus, a man of power and position, humbled himself and did the one thing he had never expected to do: he set aside his pride and fell at Jesus' feet.

In that moment, it wasn't Jairus the synagogue ruler who knelt before Jesus—it was a father, broken and desperate for a miracle. "My little daughter is at the point of death: I pray thee, come and lay thy hands on her, that she may be healed; and she shall live" (Mark 5:23, KJV). The urgency in his voice, the trembling in his plea—this was a father who had nothing left to give but his faith. It was a raw, vulnerable moment. Jairus wasn't asking for a sermon, for philosophical teachings, or for wisdom. He was asking for a touch. A healing touch.

What was left for Jairus but faith? What else could he do but believe that this man, Jesus, had the power to save his daughter? In those final moments, when everything seemed lost, Jairus had a choice: to continue in the desperation of helplessness or to place his hope in the miraculous. And so, he chose faith. He reached out, not knowing what would happen, but trusting that Jesus was the answer to his prayers.

Jesus, moved by Jairus' desperation and his faith, agreed to go with him. The two of them set off, making their way through the dense, pressing crowd. It was impossible to move quickly, the streets were full, and people pressed in from all sides. There was an air of expectancy that hung over the crowd. Some hoped to witness a miracle, others to be healed themselves, but for Jairus, this wasn't about the crowd. This was about his daughter. This was about getting Jesus to her in time.

But as they moved toward Jairus' home, something unexpected happened. An interruption. Amidst the crowd, someone else needed Jesus. Another person, another desperate soul, who had been waiting for a moment like this to come. And so, during a father's desperate journey, Jesus stopped. A woman—one who had suffered for twelve years from a bleeding condition that made her unclean—had quietly reached out and touched the hem of His garment. She, too, believed in the power of Jesus. She, too, had faith that He could heal her.

The interruption was jarring. Jairus had come for a reason, and his heart must have been in turmoil. How could this be happening now? He needed Jesus, and yet here He was, stopping to address the faith of someone else. Every moment counted. Every second that passed meant a second less to reach his daughter.

But in the chaos, Jesus did not hurry. He did not dismiss the interruption. He knew that each moment, each person, each interaction held something greater than the immediate need. Jesus understood that while Jairus' pain was real, so was the woman's. He knew that their faith needed to be nurtured. He knew that no one was overlooked, no one was unimportant. Jesus turned, spoke to the woman, and healed her, showing that in God's kingdom, no one's need was too small or insignificant to be addressed.

And then, in the midst of this moment of grace, came the news that every parent dreads: Jairus' daughter had died. *"Thy daughter is dead: why troublest thou the Master any further?"* (Mark 5:35, KJV). The words were a cold, hard slap to Jairus' heart. His worst fear had been realized. His little girl, the one he had hoped for and prayed for, was gone. How could he move forward from this? How could faith survive in the face of death?

But then Jesus, in His compassion, turned to Jairus with words that were meant to steady his heart: *"Be not afraid, only believe"* (Mark 5:36, KJV). These simple words—uttered in the face of such grief—were a lifeline. They were a reminder that faith, even in the face of the greatest tragedy, had the power to overcome. It was a call to trust in God's ability to do the impossible, to believe that death was not the end of the story.

Jairus could have chosen to turn away, to give in to despair, to believe that death had the final say. But instead, he chose to believe. He chose to trust Jesus, to hold onto the hope that even in the darkest of moments, God's power could still break through.

When they arrived at Jairus' home, the mourners were already gathered. The wailing and weeping filled the room, the air heavy with sorrow. It was a sound that marked the end of a life, the finality of death. But Jesus, undeterred by the grief that surrounded Him, spoke into that sorrow with a voice that was filled with authority and love. *"Why make ye this ado, and weep? the damsel is not dead, but sleepeth"* (Mark 5:39, KJV).

The mourners laughed at Him, scoffing at the idea that a little girl could be anything but dead. To them, death was the inevitable conclusion of life. But Jesus was about to reveal that in His presence, death was not the final word. He was about to show them that there was a power beyond the grave, a life that could overcome even death itself.

Jesus took the child's parents and His closest disciples into the room where the girl lay. There, in the quiet stillness, surrounded by grief and disbelief, Jesus spoke to the girl's soul with tenderness and authority: "Talitha cumi," which means, *"Damsel, I say unto thee, arise"* (Mark 5:41, KJV). These words were not spoken to the body, but to the very essence of life that had been taken from her. In that moment, Jesus did not merely revive the child; He called her back to life with the voice of God.

And then, in an instant, the girl arose.

She didn't just stir or shift in her bed. She rose. And with that moment, the room was filled with astonishment, awe, and overwhelming joy. The mourners who had laughed at Jesus now stood in stunned silence, unable to comprehend the miracle that had just occurred. Jairus, whose heart had been shattered, looked on in disbelief as his daughter, restored and whole, stood before him. The miracle had come to pass. His faith had been rewarded.

As a mother, I can only imagine the overwhelming relief, the unspeakable joy that Jairus must have felt as he looked at his daughter, alive and well. The grief, the fear, the sense of helplessness—all vanished in that instant, replaced by a joy that no words could contain. His faith had triumphed, and in doing so, he had witnessed a miracle that would forever change his life.

This moment, though it seemed to be an interruption in Jesus' journey, was in fact the moment where faith triumphed over death. It was a testimony that no situation—no matter how dire—could limit the power of God. Death itself was not beyond Jesus' reach. What Jairus had feared most—the loss of his daughter—had become the very catalyst for the display of God's glory.

For Jairus, this interruption became a moment of grace. His faith was tested, but it was also rewarded with the restoration of his daughter. In the face of loss, there was life. In the shadow of death, there was resurrection. And through it all, the love of a father for his child, combined with his faith in Jesus, became the very means by which God's power was made manifest.

As mothers, we can relate to Jairus in ways that go beyond his faith in that moment. The depth of a mother's love and her hope for her children is immeasurable. We, too, live in a world where we see death in many forms—loss of health, loss of opportunities, loss of hope. But this story reminds us that in the face of loss, Jesus offers life. It calls us to hold on to faith, to believe even when everything around us seems to say otherwise. Jairus' story is not just about the power of Jesus; it's a reflection of the hope that a mother's heart can hold—even in the darkest of times. And it calls us to remember that in every interruption, there may be a moment of grace waiting to unfold.

Read: Mark 5:35-36

Ruminate: What do you do when you face moments of fear or uncertainty as a mother? How do you respond when you feel that all hope is lost?

Jesus told Jairus not to fear and to believe. How can you apply this message in your own life, especially when you are overwhelmed or uncertain about the future?

In moments of chaos or fear, where do you place your faith? How can you turn your fears into opportunities to trust in God's ability to work in impossible situations?

React: When you face a fear or challenge in your motherhood journey, take a moment today to speak out in faith: "I will not fear; I will believe." In those moments of uncertainty or when it feels like hope is slipping away, remember that Jesus offers us the same invitation—to trust Him with the impossible. Let your faith rise above the fear and watch for God's grace to work in even the most difficult situations.

8

◎◈◈◈◈

Interruption in the Synagogue

Interruption in the Synagogue

Jesus' ministry in Capernaum was not only marked by the miraculous healings and profound teachings that rippled through the streets but was also deeply intertwined with the sacred space of the synagogue, the heart of Jewish worship and religious practice. For the people of Capernaum, the synagogue represented a place of refuge—a space where order and tradition held sway, where prayer was offered, and where the reading of Scripture shaped the rhythm of daily life. It was within these walls that they sought to deepen their faith and understanding of God. But on one particular Sabbath, as Jesus entered the synagogue to teach, that peaceful sanctuary would become the site of a dramatic interruption—an event that would shake the very foundations of their understanding of God's power.

As a mother, I often find myself navigating the delicate balance between the comforting routine of daily life and the sudden, unexpected interruptions that can change everything. There are days when it feels as though I have everything in control, the rhythm of our home, the cadence of meals, and the routine of bedtime prayers. But then, out of nowhere, an unexpected situation arisen interruption. An urgent call, an unexpected illness, or a problem that cannot be ignored. In those moments, everything I thought I knew about managing my life, my family, and my home is disrupted, and I am forced to confront the unexpected.

In the same way, the peaceful Sabbath gathering in the synagogue was about to be interrupted. Jesus, as He had done countless times before, began to teach the crowd, speaking of the kingdom of God—the life He came to offer, the new way of living and seeing the world that was found in Him. The people who had gathered in the synagogue likely came with a certain expectation: that the Sabbath would follow its usual rhythm of prayer, scripture reading, and quiet reflection. But as Jesus spoke, something remarkable and unsettling happened. An interruption, one that would change the course of the gathering, broke through the calm.

A man in the congregation—likely someone known to the community—began shouting, his voice filled with raw fear and aggression. His words pierced the serene atmosphere: *"Let us alone; what have we to do with thee, thou Jesus of Nazareth? Art thou come to destroy us? I know thee who thou art, the Holy One of God!"* (Mark 1:24, KJV). These words, shocking and full of terror, did not come from the man himself, but from the unclean spirit that possessed him. It was an interruption that came not from the man's own voice but from the darkness within him—an unholy cry that broke the stillness of the moment.

For the people of Capernaum, this was no ordinary disruption. This moment was charged with spiritual significance. The synagogue, a place where the Jewish people sought to encounter God and draw near to Him, became a battleground. It was no longer just a space where prayers were offered, or the law was read. In that moment, it became the stage for a confrontation between the kingdom of God and the forces of evil. The man who had been possessed, likely known to the community for his troubled state, was no longer just a passive observer in the background. His very presence became a symbol of the spiritual darkness that Jesus had come to confront.

In the first-century Jewish context, a person who was possessed by an unclean spirit was not only seen as spiritually defiled but was often excluded from the community. They were marginalized and pushed to the edges of society. The synagogue, which should have been a place of healing and restoration, was instead a place where such individuals were often isolated. This man, whose identity had been overshadowed by the unclean spirit within him, had likely been cast aside by society—relegated to the periphery, beyond the reach of normal healing or restoration. His impurity was a visible sign of the brokenness of the world, and he was seen as a reflection of that which was beyond redemption.

But Jesus, in His infinite compassion and power, was about to shatter these cultural and religious boundaries. His response to the man's outburst was not one of fear, hesitation, or confusion. Instead, it was a response of absolute authority. Jesus did not simply offer a prayer for healing. He spoke directly to the unclean spirit within the man, commanding it with divine authority: *"Hold thy peace, and come out of him" (Mark 1:25, KJV).* In that moment, Jesus spoke with the kind of power that left no room for doubt. His command was clear and unambiguous. The unclean spirit had no choice but to obey, and the man convulsed in distress as the spirit was driven out, leaving the man free from its oppression.

The crowd that had gathered in the synagogue stood in stunned silence. They had never witnessed anything like this before. The synagogue, usually reserved for the reading of Scripture and the study of the law, had become the stage for an extraordinary event—a direct confrontation between the forces of good and evil. The people were in awe, whispering to one another in astonishment: *"What thing is this? What new doctrine is this? For with authority commandeth He even the unclean spirits, and they do obey Him" (Mark 1:27, KJV).* Their words revealed the magnitude of what they had just witnessed. This was not a simple healing or an ordinary teaching moment. Jesus had demonstrated a divine power, one that transcended the normal boundaries of the synagogue and Jewish law. He was not just a teacher. He was the Holy One of God, sent to bring deliverance to the oppressed and to confront the powers of darkness.

For the people of Capernaum, this moment was not only a revelation of Jesus' authority but also a profound challenge to their understanding of God's kingdom. In the eyes of the religious leaders of the time, the man possessed by the unclean spirit was beyond redemption. He was seen as spiritually unclean and excluded from the community's religious life. The established religious system, with its laws and rituals, was designed to maintain purity and exclusion, and the man's impurity made him an outcast. But Jesus' act of deliverance turned this understanding on its head. His authority was not bound by the rules and rituals that governed religious purity. His power was not confined to the synagogue or to the boundaries of Jewish law. Instead, Jesus came to bring freedom to the oppressed, to heal the broken, and to restore those who had been cast aside.

The implications of this miracle were far-reaching. For the religious leaders, it was a direct challenge to their system of purity, exclusion, and rituals. The act of Jesus confronting the unclean spirit in the synagogue undermined the religious hierarchy and its strict boundaries. In their view, the man possessed by the spirit was not worthy of inclusion in the community of faith. But Jesus demonstrated that the kingdom of God did not operate on such principles. It was not a kingdom of exclusion but one of inclusion, one where even the most marginalized and spiritually oppressed could find healing and restoration.

For the man himself, this moment of deliverance was nothing short of dramatic. No longer would he be defined by the darkness that had oppressed him. No longer would he be a figure of ridicule or scorn. In an instant, he was restored—not just physically, but spiritually and socially as well. His healing brought him back into the fold of the community, no longer an outcast but a person made whole by the power of Jesus.

For the people of Capernaum, this interruption in the synagogue marked the beginning of a new understanding of God's kingdom. It was not a kingdom that was confined to religious rituals or sacred spaces. It was a kingdom that transcended boundaries, that reached into the lives of the marginalized, the broken, and the oppressed. Jesus had shown them that God's kingdom was not about maintaining the status quo but about bringing restoration to all people, regardless of their social, spiritual, or physical state.

As the people left the synagogue that day, they were filled with awe, but they were also left with a new understanding of who Jesus was and what He had come to do. They had witnessed firsthand that Jesus was not just a teacher or a rabbi. He was the embodiment of the kingdom of God on earth—a kingdom where the unclean were made clean, the broken were restored, and the oppressed were set free. And for many of them, their lives would never be the same again.

This miracle in the synagogue was a powerful reminder that Jesus came to challenge the established norms and to confront the powers of darkness. It was a moment of interruption, but it was also a moment of grace. Through this miracle, Jesus revealed the authority of God's kingdom and demonstrated that the power of God is greater than any force that seeks to oppress, exclude, or destroy. And in that moment, the lives of the people of Capernaum were forever changed.

Read: Mark 1:21-28, Luke 4:31-37, Matthew 12:22-29, Isaiah 61:1-3, Luke 11:20-22

Ruminate: What does it mean for us today that Jesus has authority over the spiritual forces of darkness?

How does this event challenge our understanding of the role of the church in dealing with spiritual oppression in the world?

How can we, as believers, be agents of deliverance and healing in our own communities?

In what ways do we allow spiritual darkness to have a voice in our lives, and how can we invite Jesus to speak with His authority into these areas?

What are the social and religious boundaries that we need to confront in our own understanding of God's grace and power?

React: Like the man in the synagogue, many today are held captive by forces of darkness—whether they are spiritual, emotional, or relational. Jesus' authority over the unclean spirit in the synagogue is a reminder that no one is beyond the reach of God's grace. As the body of Christ, we are called to carry that authority into the world, bringing deliverance and healing to those who are oppressed. Let us not shy away from the uncomfortable or the unconventional but boldly proclaim the power of Christ to interrupt the forces of darkness and bring light into every shadow.

9

Grace Unmeasured

Grace Unmeasured

There are moments in life when everything feels in its proper place. The rhythm of the day flows smoothly, a sense of balance and peace has been carefully cultivated. I can't help but imagine Jesus, in the wake of the news of John the Baptist's death, seeking a quiet moment—an opportunity to grieve, to process, to replenish His strength. As mothers, we understand that sometimes all we need is a brief respite—an interlude before we face the next challenge. A space to gather our thoughts, to regain our composure, and to center ourselves again. It is a longing familiar to every heart overwhelmed by the demands of the day, the steady cadence of responsibilities, and the relentless call for attention.

But as anyone who has tried to rest knows, life rarely cooperates. In Jesus' case, it wasn't a crying baby or a toddler's tantrum that interrupted His grief—it was a multitude. A great crowd, filled with hunger not just for food but for healing, for hope, and for the words that would offer them a vision of life beyond their struggles. It was a reminder that no matter how we plan or structure our days, interruptions often come with a force far greater than we can imagine. And when the need is this vast, the weight of it can feel overwhelming.

I, too, have faced those days when the load seems impossibly heavy, when I feel like there's no way I can meet all the needs that pull at me. Whether it's my children, my responsibilities, or the people in my life, there are moments when I wish I could escape, even for just a few minutes, to catch my breath. The disciples, in the face of the same kind of overwhelming demand, saw what needed to be done. The people had followed them far into the wilderness, and now they were hungry—famished, even. The day was nearing its end, and the nearest village was miles away. The disciples, ever practical, suggested a solution: "Send them away," they said, *"let them go buy food for themselves"* (Matthew 14:15).

I've had moments like this, when the task at hand feels insurmountable, when I can't see how I can meet the need that is before me. It's easy to look at what's lacking and feel like we simply don't have enough to offer. How can I, with my limited energy, patience, and wisdom, meet the needs of those entrusted to me? Sometimes, the weight of responsibility feels like too much. But here, Jesus doesn't offer the easy answer. He doesn't tell the disciples to cut their losses or to send the crowd away. Instead, He does something entirely different: He invites the interruption. *"They need not depart; give ye them to eat"* (Matthew 14:16).

It's a response that challenges our way of thinking. Jesus doesn't see scarcity; He sees opportunity. The disciples, looking at the meager resources available—five loaves of bread and two fish, couldn't imagine how it could possibly suffice for the thousands gathered before them. It seemed ridiculous, almost cruel, to think that such a small amount could feed so many. And yet, Jesus saw something that they could not: He saw the potential of what they had. He knew that when placed in His hands, that small offering would be enough.

As a mother, I've often looked at my life and felt the same way—the way Jesus saw the disciples in that moment. There have been countless times when I've looked at my exhaustion, my lack of resources, and felt like I had nothing left to give. I've asked, "How can I do it all? How can I possibly meet the needs of my children, my spouse, my family, my job, and my own heart?" But just as Jesus did with the loaves and fish, He takes our meager offerings and multiplies them. He sees the small things we give—whether it's a prayer whispered in the quiet of the morning, a moment of patience during chaos, or a small act of kindness—and He transforms them into something greater than we could ever imagine.

In this moment, Jesus invites the disciples to bring what they have, no matter how insufficient it may seem. He takes the loaves and fish, blesses them, and begins to break them. And then a miracle happens. What began as an impossibly small offering—barely enough for the disciples themselves—was multiplied. The bread and fish didn't run out. The people were fed, and not only that, but they were also satisfied. When the meal was over, there were twelve baskets of leftovers, far more than they could have hoped for. Five loaves and two fish became an abundance, more than enough to feed thousands.

As a mother, I see this not only as a story about food but as a profound illustration of how Jesus meets our limitations with grace. There have been days when I felt stretched beyond measure, when I could barely scrape together enough energy or patience to get through the day. And yet, in those moments, Jesus shows up. He multiplies what little I have—whether it's the love I must give, the energy I can muster, or the time I have to spare. Just as the small offering of bread and fish became a feast, so too do my small efforts in His hands become more than I could have imagined.

This miracle also challenges our conventional thinking about scarcity. In a world where resources are often limited, where it feels like there is never enough, Jesus shows us that in His kingdom, grace and provision overflow. I think about the times my children have looked up at me with expectant eyes, hoping for something more than I can give, and yet I do my best, trusting that God will provide what's needed. This is the same grace that Jesus offers to those who come in need. He doesn't tell them to work harder or earn their place at the table. He simply gives—and not just a little, but in abundance.

In Jesus' time, meals were often reserved for the wealthy or powerful. They were exclusive events, meant for those who had status or influence. But in this moment, Jesus broke down those social and cultural boundaries. He invited everyone to the table. The fishermen, the farmers, the poor, and the marginalized—each one was welcomed. And as a mother, I can't help but think about the times when I've had to stretch a meal to make sure everyone has enough, pulling out an extra plate when it seemed there wouldn't be enough to go around. There's something beautiful in that—something that reflects the heart of God, who takes what little we have and makes it enough.

The disciples, too, were confronted with their own doubts and limitations. They couldn't see how this small offering could possibly meet the overwhelming need. But by the end of the day, they were witnesses to a miracle. They saw the loaves and fish multiplied, not just enough to meet the need, but more than enough. There were leftovers—twelve baskets full. The small offering they had given had been transformed into an abundant feast. It's a reminder that even when we feel we are running on empty, Jesus takes our small acts of love, our moments of patience, and our tired hearts, and He multiplies them in ways we can't always see.

At the end of the day, when the crowd had eaten their fill and the baskets were collected, I imagine the disciples standing in awe of what had just happened. What had started as a simple need—hunger—had turned into an overwhelming display of grace. The leftovers didn't just fill the gap; they overflowed. Twelve baskets full. And as I reflect on my own life, I think about how, in the moments when I feel I don't have enough, God is working in the background to make His grace overflow in ways that I might never understand.

The feeding of the five thousand is a reminder to me that in the kingdom of God, there is no shortage. There is always enough. There is always grace. There is always abundance. When we offer what little we have—whether it's our time, our energy, or our love—Jesus takes it, blesses it, and multiplies it. In a world that often feels like it's running on empty, this miracle is a reminder that in Jesus' hands, even our smallest offerings can become a feast for many.

So, like the disciples, I am invited to bring my offering—no matter how small—and trust that in the hands of Jesus, it will be more than enough. He is the God of abundance, the one who takes our little and makes it overflow, feeding not just our bodies but our souls. In a world full of scarcity, He shows us that grace is unmeasured, overflowing, and more than enough for all.

Read: Matthew 14:13-21, John 6:5-13

Ruminate: Jesus saw the deep need of the people and responded with compassion, not just addressing their hunger but their deeper longing. How can we reflect this same compassion in our daily lives to meet both physical and spiritual needs?

The disciples focused on their lack of resources, asking, "Where can we buy bread?" But Jesus showed them that true provision comes from Him. How often do you feel limited by your circumstances, and how can you trust Jesus with your limitations, knowing He can multiply even the smallest offering?

Jesus provided not just enough, but more than enough—an overflow that reflects God's grace. How have you experienced God's abundant grace in your life, and how can you share that abundance with others?

Jesus broke down societal barriers by providing for everyone, regardless of status. How does this miracle challenge your views on community, and how can you foster a more inclusive environment that reflects Jesus' radical hospitality?

React: Bring your small offerings—time, talents, or resources—to Jesus today, trusting that He can multiply them for His glory and the benefit of others. Be an instrument of God's grace to others by meeting their spiritual and emotional needs through acts of kindness, sharing the gospel, or simply being present. Surrender any areas of lack or limitation in your life to Jesus, trusting that He will provide abundantly in ways beyond your expectations. Work to break down the walls of division in your community by embracing the inclusive, radical hospitality of Jesus and reflecting His love and acceptance to all.

10

Grace in the Interruptions

Grace in the Interruptions

Motherhood is a life marked by interruptions, and those interruptions come in all shapes and sizes. From a sudden cry that shatters the silence of a peaceful moment to a spilled cup of juice in the middle of an important meeting, or the constant tug of little hands demanding attention even when we long for just a moment of rest. But what if we began to see these interruptions not as burdens, but as invitations to experience the miraculous? What if these moments of disruption could be the very spaces where God's grace meets us?

In the life of Jesus, we see a Savior whose ministry was constantly interrupted. His days were filled with people bringing urgent needs, sick bodies seeking healing, lonely hearts desiring companionship, and hungry souls hoping for sustenance. Yet in every interruption, Jesus responded with compassion, grace, and power. His miracles didn't happen according to a scheduled plan; they were often unexpected moments when the needs of others collided with His purpose on earth.

The life of a mother reflects this in so many ways. We find ourselves living in a rhythm that is frequently broken by the needs of our children, our families, and our communities. Yet, as we saw in the previous chapters, these interruptions are not random disruptions in the grand story of God's plan. They are, in fact, sacred moments where His grace can flow freely. In the midst of chaos, we are invited to experience His power, His compassion, and His unending love.

One of the most beautiful aspects of Jesus' miracles is how they often happened in response to interruptions. Consider the woman with the issue of blood, the desperate father seeking healing for his child, or the man who couldn't hear or speak. Each miracle occurred because someone reached out to Jesus in their moment of need, and in each instance, He didn't see their needs as inconveniences but as opportunities to display God's grace and power.

As mothers, we must hold this perspective close to our hearts. Each interruption in our lives is not an obstacle to be overcome but an opportunity to experience God's grace in action. Just as Jesus paused to heal the sick, feed the hungry, and restore the broken, we too are called to pause during motherhood's chaos and recognize the sacredness of these moments. These are opportunities for grace to abound.

A SHIFT IN PERSPECTIVE: FROM BURDEN TO BLESSING

It's easy for a mother to feel overwhelmed by constant interruptions. The phone rings just when you're in the middle of a project. A toddler needs a snack right when you sit down to eat. The to-do list never seems to shrink. Life pulls at you from every direction, and it can feel as though you're constantly meeting everyone else's needs, with little left for yourself.

But what if we began to see these moments not as burdens, but as invitations to experience God's grace? What if, like Jesus, we learned to embrace the interruptions, knowing that in each one, God's love and power are at work? Jesus didn't turn away from the needs that surrounded Him; He saw each one as an opportunity to reflect the heart of God. As mothers, we are invited to do the same. When our lives feel stretched thin, when we're tired and weary, we can trust that in these moments, God is refining us, growing us, and revealing His grace in beautiful ways.

Think about the times when you've felt most overwhelmed—those long nights with a sick child or the never-ending cycle of cleaning, cooking, and caring. It's easy to lose sight of the fact that these moments are often where God does His most transformative work. During the mess and chaos, He is shaping our hearts, building our character, and deepening our understanding of His love.

THE POWER OF JESUS' COMPASSION

Throughout His ministry, Jesus was deeply moved by the needs of others. He didn't view them as interruptions but as divine appointments. His heart was moved with compassion for the sick, the broken, and the lost. His response was always one of grace, kindness, and love.

As mothers, we too are called to this deep compassion. The constant demands of motherhood can leave us feeling exhausted, empty, and sometimes even resentful of the interruptions. Yet, just as Jesus ministered out of a well of deep compassion, we can, too. God's grace is not something we muster up on our own; it's something He pours into us. When we're weary, when we feel like we have nothing left to give, God's grace fills us, allowing us to respond to our children with patience, love, and understanding.

This doesn't mean motherhood is always easy. It's not. But it does mean that we don't have to rely on our own strength. When we lean into God's grace, trusting that He will provide what we need, we can begin to see the interruptions as opportunities to reflect His love. Just as Jesus was able to pause and show compassion to the crowds, we too can pause and show compassion to our children, knowing that in doing so, we are emulating Christ's love.

THE MINISTRY OF PRESENCE: JESUS AS OUR MODEL

One of the most profound aspects of Jesus' ministry was His ability to be fully present, even amid His busy life. He didn't rush through His encounters or hurry His miracles. He took the time to listen, to care, and to fully engage with those in need. His presence was a gift to those around Him, and it was transformative.

As mothers, we are often pulled in many directions, our attention divided among countless tasks. But Jesus offers us a beautiful example of what it means to be present. We may not always have hours of uninterrupted time with our children, but we can give them the gift of our attention. When they call out in need, we can stop, look them in the eyes, and be fully present. In those moments, we are offering them the same kind of love and attention that Jesus offers us.

THE MIRACLES OF JESUS AND THE MIRACLES OF MOTHERHOOD

Throughout this study, we've seen that Jesus' miracles were often interruptions in His ministry. Each one was a moment when grace overflowed—whether it was healing the sick, feeding the hungry, or comforting the broken. These interruptions weren't burdens; they were opportunities for God's kingdom to break into the world.

As mothers, we can see our own interruptions as opportunities to bring God's grace into the everyday moments of motherhood. When our children cry out for attention, when our routines are disrupted, we can respond with the love and grace that Jesus demonstrated. Just as Jesus brought the kingdom of God to earth through His miracles, we, too, can bring God's kingdom into the lives of our children through our responses to the interruptions in our lives.

FINDING GRACE IN THE INTERRUPTIONS

The key to finding grace in the interruptions of motherhood is remembering that these moments are not accidents. God has placed us in the lives of our children for a purpose, and each interruption is an opportunity to live out that purpose with grace. We may not always understand why things happen the way they do, but we can trust that God is at work in the midst of it all.

When we look at the interruptions through the lens of God's grace, we can find beauty in the mess, peace in the chaos, and joy in the frustration. Just as Jesus responded with grace to the interruptions in His ministry, we can respond with grace in our own lives.

Motherhood is a journey full of interruptions. But it is also a journey full of grace. As we embrace the interruptions, we embrace the opportunity to experience God's grace more deeply and to become vessels of that grace to those around us.

A FINAL WORD

As we finish this reflection, I invite you to pause and think about the miracles of Jesus we've explored together. Consider how He responded to interruptions—not with frustration or impatience, but with grace and compassion. Then, think about how you can respond to the interruptions in your own life in the same way. Each moment is an invitation to experience God's grace, to grow in patience, and to reflect His love. Motherhood is a calling—a sacred, high calling. And in every interruption, you are living that calling with grace. May you continue to find strength, peace, and joy in the moments of disruption, knowing that in those very moments, God's grace is at work in you and through you.

Read: Mark 6:31

Ruminate: How do you react to the "interruptions" of motherhood?

What would it look like if we embraced the interruptions, and allowed them to be moments for God's presence to show up in our lives?

In the busy moments of your day, when you feel overwhelmed by the demands of motherhood, how can you seek rest in God's presence, even in the middle of the chaos?

React: Pause for a moment today and embrace an interruption—whether it's a moment of silence with your child, a small act of kindness, or a moment of reflection amid chaos. Take this as an opportunity to remember that God's grace often meets us in the interruptions, and it is through these moments that we grow, reflect, and experience His presence more fully.

www.ingramcontent.com/pod-product-compliance
Lightning Source LLC
Chambersburg PA
CBHW060254150626
46553CB00019BA/2277